I FEEL SAD

By Katie Kawa

Gareth Stevens
Publishing

Please visit our website, www.garethstevens.com. For a free color catalog of all our high-quality books, call toll free 1-800-542-2595 or fax 1-877-542-2596.

Library of Congress Cataloging-in-Publication Data

Kawa, Katie.
 I feel sad / Katie Kawa.
     p. cm. — (How do I feel?)
 Includes index.
 ISBN 978-1-4339-8120-3 (pbk.)
 ISBN 978-1-4339-8121-0 (6-pack)
 ISBN 978-1-4339-8119-7 (library binding)
 1. Sadness in children–Juvenile literature. I. Title.
 BF723.S15K39 2013
 152.4—dc23
                                      2012019212

First Edition

Published in 2013 by
Gareth Stevens Publishing
111 East 14th Street, Suite 349
New York, NY 10003

Editor: Katie Kawa
Designer: Mickey Harmon

Printed in the United States of America

CPSIA compliance information: Batch #CW13GS: For further information contact Gareth Stevens, New York, New York at 1-800-542-2595.

Contents

I am moving
to a new town.
My dad has
a new job there.

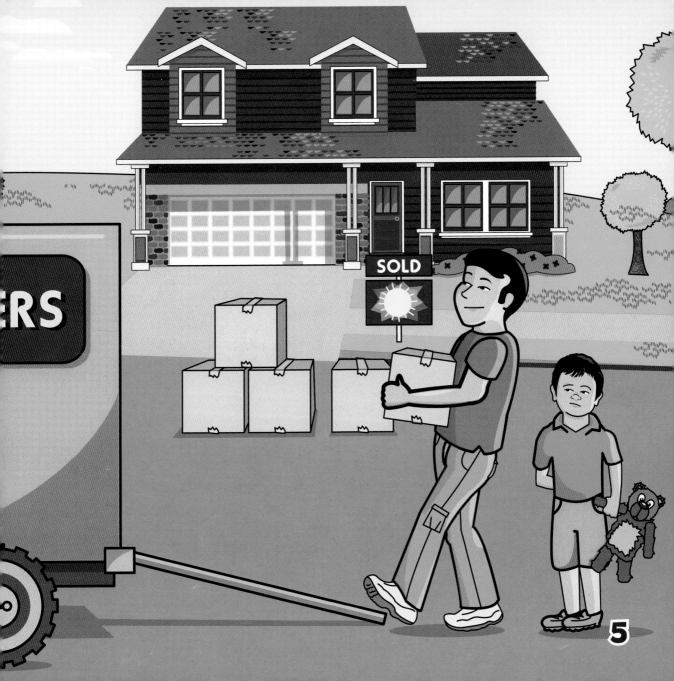

I do not want
to leave my town.
I feel sad.

I have to say goodbye
to my best friend.
Her name is Morgan.

9

It makes me sad
to say goodbye
to Morgan.

I cry because I am sad.

Then, my dad hugs me.

My family and I drive
to our new town.
Movers help us bring our
things to our new house.

I do not know any kids
in my new town.
This makes me feel sad.

19

Then, I meet friends
at my new school.
I do not feel sad anymore.

Morgan visits me
at my new house.
Now I feel happy!

23

Words to Know

friend

movers

Index